I0465830

Living and working in China

Julie Woodman

Copyright © 2018 ChatterBox English

All rights reserved.

UNDERSTANDING CULTURE

Understanding cultural differences is one of the most important skills that organisations require in the 21st century. As business is becoming more global, the need for manager and teams to have a good understanding of cultural differences will enable them to work more effectively and innovatively. Whether you are working within your home culture within a culturally diverse team or working in a different culture, understanding the key values of different cultures will have a positive effect on you, your team and your organisation.

This book focuses on Chinese culture, and provides a good insight into the key values, expectations and social requirements for anyone wishing to live and work in the China, work for a Chinese company or work within a team with Chinese nationals.

The Chinese culture belongs not only to the Chinese,

But also to the whole world.

All things are difficult before they are easy

A friend to everyone is a friend to no one

Moving Countries

Moving to another country or working with people from a different country is very difficult, but also one of the most requested skills in the 21st century.

The anxiety and stress of Culture shock is well recognised amongst those relocating but is also becoming increasingly evident amongst those working within multi-cultural teams.

How you cope with culture shock will have a big impact on your future.

There are the obvious differences of language, location, weather, laws and food. But the real differences between social rules can be far reaching from finding childcare, getting your electric connected, or to knowing what to do in an emergency.

In a work environment, do you know what your boss will expect of you, how negotiations occur, the protocol for information sharing or how to give feedback.

This guide gives the basic information on the unique cultural elements within the country, to help you understand the key values of the nationals

CULTURAL OVERVIEW

Mindset

A set of assumptions or notions that are held by one or a group of people. it is so powerful that it is able to adapt and change behaviours. It is difficult to counteract the effect that mindset has on decision making and understanding.

- China is still a Communist country, despite the international pressure that has been place upon it.
- It is looking for modernisation but is not interested westernisation.
- Authority is accepted and not criticised.
- Equality is wanted.
- The thought that everyone would have a job for life is accepted less in the current economic climate.
- The biggest priority in china is to care for the family.
- A growing number of Chinese are living below the poverty line.
- Most people in china are ethnic Chinese
- They have a huge range of languages within the country.

Characteristics of society

Societies need populations within which social relationships can be formed. To create these relationships, societies require: A sense of likeness, Differences to establish respect, Interdependence, Cooperation, Conflict, Change, Culture

- China has the world's largest population.
- Chinese population is currently 1.3 billion, growing almost every second (2017)
- Chinese population is over 18% of the total world population.
- There are approximately 150 people per KM2.
- Their land total is 9,390.784 km2
- 59.1% of the population live in an urban environment.
- The average age in china is 37.3 years (2017)
- There are 55 ethnic groups in China.
- The Han Chinese represent over 91% of the population (1.2 billion) in 2010.
- Other groups include Zhuang, Uyghur, Hui, Manchu, Miao, Yi, Tujia, Tibetan and Mongol.
- The individual has little power or privacy.
- For many years families were limited to one child, but this has created an unbalanced society.
- Many Chinese are religious – Confucianism being the primary religion.
- China is officially an atheist country.
- Highly educated.
- Low divorce rate but rising rapidly.
- Living standards among the middle classes are improving.
- Living standards among the working classes are still very poor.
- Average life expectancy 75 years.
- A male dominated society.
- Open discrimination against women.

Discrimination

The unjust or prejudicial treatment of different categories of people, especially on the grounds of race, age, or sex.

- There is less discrimination within the major cities.
- Women are still discriminated against.
- Women in business are accepted but they have a more difficult time being accepted.
- Chinese businesswomen are slowly being recognised within the major cities.
- Homosexuality is not illegal in China, however many are still 'encouraged' to have heterosexual relationships.
- The mass media do not discuss homosexuality or pornography.
- Those with disabilities are protected within Chinese society.
- Humanitarianism protects the rights of people with disabilities, although human rights in general are not respected.
- Those with disabilities are expected to contribute to society and therefore receive all the expected economic and social rewards.
- Children with disabilities are educated by the state.
- Human rights are a major concern for the international community.
- Religious practitioners, political activists etc are treated badly by the state.
- Freedom of speech and freedom of expression are restricted.
- Facebook, twitter, etc are blocked in china.

Language

The official languages in china are:

- Mandarin
- Cantonese
- English
- Portuguese.

There are 56 recognised ethnic languages in China

- Standard mandarin is spoken by over 70% of the population.
- Tibetan is the main language in Tibet.
- Mongolian is the main language in inner Mongolia.
- Hong Kong's main language is Cantonese and English
- Macau speaks mainly Portuguese.
- Mandarin is used as the common language between different areas of the country.

China has more languages than the whole of Europe, but since the end of the Qing dynasty there has been an aim for one common language – Putonghua/Mandarin. There are still Eight major language groups within China including:
Mandarin – 800m (Northern/Beijing/Sichuan)
Yue – 70m (Cantonese - Guangdong)
Wu – 90m (Shanghainese)
Min – Spoken in Taiwan/Hainan Gan/Hakka/Xiang
Cantonese - spoken in Southern China and Hong Kong.

Most of China speaks Mandarin, rather than the very differently spoken Cantonese, even though when written both these languages are almost linguistically identical.

Chinese characters are commonplace throughout China, and have the same meaning, but the figures are pronounced in very different ways. Chinese has approximately 50,000 characters, with an average of 8,000 in common use.

'Yang Guizi' is how foreign 'devils' (i.e. foreigners) are referred to in Mandarin. For Cantonese speakers, the term 'Gwei Lo' is used. Neither term is polite but they are not necessarily derogatory, but more 'street' language.

Population

Age Range

- 0 – 14 years   17%
- 15 – 24 years 13.27%
- 25 – 54 years 48.42%
- 55 – 64 years 10.87%
- 65+ years 10.35%

Life Expectancy

- Expectancy is 75.15 years
- Life expectancy for men is 73.09 years
- Life expectancy for women is 77.43

Ethnic Breakdown

- Han Chinese   91.6%
- Zhuang   1.3 %
- Others   7.1%

Diversity

- China has more than 56 ethnic groups
- Han Chinese are almost 92% of the country
- Diversity is not protected by the government
- China is a male dominated society
- After the cultural revolution women became less discriminated against
- Woman are now found in business and within some high-ranking positions
- However, job adverts still discriminate over jobs for women and jobs for men
- Diversity policies within the workplace are usually only found in multinational companies
- Equality is more common in cities. Discrimination is still high in rural areas.
- Foreign businesswomen can have difficulties in being accepted
- Homosexuality is tolerated but not really accepted. Many live within heterosexual relationships
- Homosexuality and pornography are taboo subject for the media, and generate general negativity
- The Chinese disabled persons federation promotes human rights and humanitarianism amongst disabled people
- They often have equal participation in society, contributing to economic and social development
- There is workplace equal opportunities quota system for disabled employees. And special education for children if required.
- Human rights are restricted in china

- Activists for democracy are consistently harassed and detained.
- Restricted activities include religious beliefs, freedom of association, expression and the role of the media.
- Social media networks such as twitter, Facebook, you tube and Instagram are blocked by china.
- Google is blocked in China.

Beliefs

- An atheist society but allows religious freedom
- The three main faiths are Confucianism, Buddhism and Taoism
- There are 20 – 25 million Muslims.
- There are an unknown number of Christians.

Confucianism

- Confucianism has been in China since 200BC.
- It encourages traditional values of harmony, order, humaneness and benevolence, believing that this can be attained by strict hierarchies, role relations and moral principle.
- 'Li' is its code of conduct and rules of duty.

Buddhism

- Buddhism reached China at the end of 100BC
- It has adapted well to Chinese society – i.e. Nirvana means perfection rather than its original extinction and is highlighted and achieved through meditation and social withdrawal.

Taoism

- Taoism was developed by Lao Tzu
- It is both religious and philosophical.
- Achieving harmony and self-fulfilment should be done by the 'natural way'.
- It promotes humility, passivity and non-aggressive behaviours.
- It works on a live and let live basis and patience.

Lifestyle and aspirations

Aspirations – are long term goals that motivate people. Motivation is very complex, but being part of a group improves motivation, and increases the changes of achieving your aspirations. The fear of being punished, gaining acceptance and approval from your peer group, and maintaining a certain level all impact group aspirations.

Free time and leisure interests are a relatively new concept in modern day China. Some of the new hobbies are:

- Traditional games like cards and Maj Jong
- Sightseeing Chinese attractions like the Great Wall, the Yangtze River gorges, the Summer Palace and the Terracotta Army.
- Walking and hiking
- Skiing

- Ice skating and ice hockey
- Amusement parks
- Eating out – McDonalds and KFC are still quite new to the area
- Cinema - Fung Fu and romance films, although many are still censored.
- Sports, such as Gymnastics, table tennis, volleyball and basketball
- Practicing Tai Chi in public areas.
- Watching TV and there are over 3000 different channels with more than 200 run by Chinese Central Television.
- Ballroom and disco dancing
- Karaoke is popular although patriotic songs are promoted.
- Chinese circus and opera.
- Visiting the zoo, which usually have excellent conservation programmes.
- Shopping, especially for big brands.

Education

- 95.1% of the country are literate – 73% male and 77% female.
- Education is highly regarded in China and is compulsory for nine years.
- Learning is often by rote.
- Key values such as 'truth', 'kindness' and 'beauty' are taught from an early age.
- English is compulsory from Year One and is often taught in Kindergarten, from age 3.
- Primary school is from 6/7 to 11/12
- Secondary school is from 11/12 to 16
- College is for 16+.
- The number of graduates is the highest in the world being over 7 million.
- China has over 2000 universities and colleges.
- University is free and includes accommodation and grants for those who need it.
- University admissions criteria is based on academic, physical and moral qualifications.
- University enrolment rose very fast in the early 21st century, but by 2011 had begun to decrease as a result of the one child policy and easier access to foreign universities.
- Chinese education's primary aim is to train specialists for all sectors of the country's development.
- Universities and colleges offer 4 and 5 year programmes as well as the more traditional 2 and 3 years.
- After completing their first degree students are encouraged to apply to graduate schools, to advance to Masters and Doctorates.

Geography

- China covers 9,560,900 sq. km
- China is the 3rd largest, with Russia 1st and Canada 2nd
- It is placed in Eastern Asia, on the Western seaboard of the Pacific Ocean.
- North to South it covers a distance of 5,500 km and East to West is 5,000km.
- About 65% is mountainous and desert, with 13% being arable.
- China shares borders with 15 countries, including Russia, India and Korea.
- Its most northern point is on a similar latitude to Warsaw, where winter temperatures can be as low as minus 40C.
- South eastern Guangzhou is similar to Calcutta where temperatures can be plus 40C.
- China has the world's largest generating power station.
- The three Gorges Dam project has been working since 2014. It crosses the Yangtze River, is 600 feet high, 1.3 miles wide. The reservoir covers 405 square miles.

Weather and climate

The size of China has a large impact on the weather within the country.

- Northeast - Hot, dry summers with very cold winters.
- North and Central - Hot summer and cold winters, but will a very heavy annual rainfall.
- Southeast - Semi-tropical summer with cool winters, also with significant year round rainfall.

- Flooding – usually within the central, southern and western areas.
- Earthquakes - throughout the country.

Tourists prefer the weather in the spring (March/April) or Autumn (September/October).

POLITICS AND ECONOMICS

Politics

- China has been a communist country since 1949
- The constitution says that China is socialist and run by the proletariat.
- Despite moving towards capitalism, the country remains communist.
- The Chinese Communist Party (CCP), make all the major decisions within the country
- The CCP politburo and the Standing committee, headed by the General Secretary are the main decision makers within the party.
- The CCP, the government and the Military all govern the country.
- The National People's Congress (NPC) makes legislative decisions on the economy, electing high officeholders and constitutional changes.
- Membership to the NPC is for five years and they meet once a year.
- The 'Premier' is the head of government
- The 'President' is the head of State
- Neither are key decision makers
- In 1978 programmes were put in place to modernise China
- In 1989 the CCP clamped down on dissidents, and many went into hiding or fled the country.
- In 2011 programmes were put in place to rebalance the country, address inequality, but the economic slowdown has affected any outcomes for this programme.

As at 2018:

Premier – Li Keqiang

President – Xi Jinping

Economics

- Chinese economic situation has been a major success since implementation since 1978
- Chinese has the largest economy in the world
- The majority of the wealth is in state owned businesses and industries
- The private sector within China is growing
- China is a very large exporter
- Chinese tourism industry is booming
- Property booms are common in major cities, with mortgages on the increase
- China is the world's biggest producer and user of coal
- Other energy options are under development, such as hydro electricity
- Difficulties facing the Chinese economy include corruption, bureaucracy, environmental damage and unemployment.
- Poverty and low pay are still major issues within China, especially in rural areas.
- The populations continues to grow, but not sufficiently to pay for a huge aging population
- Agriculture is the biggest employer
- China produces crops and products such as rice, wheat, potatoes, corn, peanuts, cotton, oilseed, pork, fish…
- Metal mining and processing includes iron, steel, aluminium, coal fabric, petrol, chemicals etc

Cost of living

- Lower than most of the western world
- Prices are on average over 40% lower than the UK and US
- Average salary after tax 678GBP/875USD per month
- A 3 course mid-range meal for two is about 16GBP/21USD
- 1 Bed central apartment rent 393GBP/500USD per month
- Utility bills for average accommodation is 38GBP/50USD

Fiscal year

The Chinese fiscal year runs from 1st January to 31 December for all elements including the tax, statutory and planning years.

Attitudes to money

Many years of communist rule and separation from other countries has had a huge economic affect on China. Under communism, everyone had a job, became part of the associated institution, and never had to worry about income, medical care, housing, education, retirement etc, as everything was covered by their allocated role. This meant that there was little 'financial risk' involved in the lives of most Chinese nationals but was also little opportunity for advancement or change.

Now these times have ended, most nationals are becoming 'risk aware' but are also giving job security less of an overall priority. Choice of work is making people more mobile and generating more inspiration. People are moving from job to job, but also location in order to earn and/or achieve more.

Chinese people have not yet developed the materialistic nature often found in America and Europe, and spending is still very cautious within more rural areas, as these communities often still live below the poverty line.

The younger generation (post 1990), have developed more short term spending whereas the older generation are still looking further into the future.

The Chinese have a long history of gambling and, despite being illegal on the mainland, mainly people still flock to off shore locations like Hong Kong and Macau to spend vast sums of money. However, the Stock Market and National Lotteries are beginning to establish organised gambling options within China.

Money

- The currency unit is Yuan.
- Money is called RMB, which stands for Renminbi, which means 'peoples currency'.
- Notes are found in 0.10, 0.20, 0.50, 1, 2, 5, 10, 50, and 100 Yuan denominations.
- Credit cards are common, but cash is preferred in markets.
- Tipping is becoming more common in cities, where waiters expect about 12%
- Taxi drivers are not tipped.

Get up to date conversation rates from http://www.xe.com/

The Law

- Chinese law is a complicated mix of custom and statute.
- It is based on criminal law
- Its basic civil code was established in 1980 and 1987.

- Improvements on civil, administrative, criminal and commercial laws are ongoing, but this has led to a vast range of provisional laws, that are changed as soon as they become unsuitable for specific occasions.
- Even though change is ongoing to bring Chinese Law into line with international expectations, the Chinese Communist Party still heavily influences processes.
- There are over 100,000 lawyers in mainland China.
- The bigger cities have law forms led by partners, whereas the more rural areas have less established, less effective legal representation.
- Most lawyers do not provide services for feign affairs or in foreign languages.

BUSINESS

Organisational structures in China are complex and can be very difficult to understand. Many companies are state owned or affiliated. Many large organisations still include the government or ruling groups in their negotiations.

Large businesses in china run in a very different way to family owned businesses but are none the less as hierarchical as the traditional family owned business. It is important to always remember that relationships are often more important than the business proposition, and the group is much more important than any individual. See 'cultural dimensions – individual versus collective.

Guanxi

(Guanxi (/gwan shee/) is the dominating factor within Chinese business. It affects all aspects of business from simple transactions to complex international negotiations. Similar to the western networking, relationships and contacts that are made. Ensuring that you develop good relationships with the important people within your industry is vital. Also, within your specific field, you may be expected to develop relationships with extended family, local and high government officials, community groups and other groups

Honesty, and consistency is the key to success within all of these relationships. The rules of guanxi mean that everyone affected by your proposals will be consulted and re-consulted, and everyone is entitled to ask questions and give an opinion. Cultivating and encouraging these actions is the key to successful business in China. The relationship is much more important than the transaction and will affect all future involvement within the country.

Guanxi means that current relationships and 'friends' should be honoured first within the business world in China, therefore being a 'newcomer' can take a lot of time and effort to get into this networking circle.

Due to international business and requirements, government involvement is reducing.

In brief follow all laws, morals and ethics of yourself, your company, your country and also of china.

Major industries

- Toys
- Electronics
- Food processing
- Transportation
- Aircraft and space vehicles
- Telecommunications
- Minerals
- Optical and medical equipment
- Plastics

- Agriculture
- Mining and ore processing
- Machine building
- Textiles
- Apparel
- Petroleum
- Cement production
- Chemical and fertilizers
- Footwear

Imports and exports

Imports

- Over $2 trillion is imported
    - Electrical equipment
    - Machinery
    - Oil and minerals
    - Optical and medical equipment
    - Plastics
    - Organic chemicals
    - Metal ores

- They generally import from South Korea, Japan, UAS, Taiwan, Australia and Germany

Exports

- Over $2.2 trillion is exported in goods.
- China is the largest exporter in the world.
    - Electrical items
    - Machinery
    - Data processing equipment
    - Clothing
    - Textiles
    - Iron and steel
    - Optical and medical equipment

- They generally export to Hong Kong, USA, Japan and South Korea.

Workforce

- In 2016, the workforce in china accounted for approximately 71% of the population.
- China's lowest recorded workforce was 67.8% in 2010.
- There are less female workers than male workers.
- The gender gap in China is smaller than in many other countries.
- In the late 1990s the labour emphasis moved from agricultural to industrial.
- China is moving towards a more service based economy.
- Migrant worker numbers are increasing, with over 55% being under 40 years old.
- Urban wages are increasing at a faster rate than in rural areas.
- Unemployment is fairly stable at around 4%.

Ethics

- Chinese Ethics is questionable despite following the rules of Guanxi.
- Guanxi is a process of relationships and networks, whereas ethics tends to move into the legal sphere.
- State involvement affects intellectual property, banking and corruption is wide spread.
- However, this is not widely discussed.

Corporate citizenship and social responsibility

- Corporate responsibility is still a new process in china
- There is little structure or official processes for businesses to put anything back into their local community or the wider society.
- As part of guanxi or good business practice some local business have an impact of their local community or put in support or rewards for employees.
- The environment is of little concern to China, being extremely large consumers of cement, iron, steel and energy.
- Construction, fur farming and pollution are still increasing.
- China is trying to reduce its pollution levels and is leading the world in renewable energies.

Information sharing

- Information sharing is not common in China, with is being on a need- to know- basis.
- Delegation of authority is rare.
- Change is slow.
- Unless decisions will affect your work, you will not be notified.
- Team members will not be expected to ask about or question processes.
- The lack of information sharing, delegation, requesting and two way communication means that decisions can take a long time before an outcome is reached.
- This has a big impact on foreign language speakers, because unless you can understand the communication and processes in Chinese you will be unlikely to develop adequate guanxi connections.
- Withholding information is a common place way to assert power.
- Foreigners should get everything in writing.
- Use your guanxi connections to 'call in favours' if you need to know something.
- Respect company policies, your own nationalities laws and Chinese laws at all times.

Working hours and holidays

- Time in China is 8 hours ahead of GMT.
- Chinese time is often called Beijing Time.

- Although the time zone is the same all across China, Western China often has a later working day to match daylight hours.
- Business hours are normally from 8.30am to 5pm, with lunchtime closures lasting from 1 – 2 hours.
- Most Chinese business work a five day week, but many are moving to six days.
- The Labour laws state that people should not work for more than 8 hours a day, and 44 hours per week.
- Saturday and Sunday are the standard weekend days off.
- Public holidays include Chinese New Year, Qingming Festival, May Day, Dragon Boat day, Mid-autumn day, National Day and New Year's Day.

Making a good impression

- Creating a good impression revolves about building relationships and connections.
- Monitor and maintain those relationships. Effort and time are required.
- Remember relationships and trust must come before business.
- Entertain.
- Attend functions and accept offered hospitality such as eating out, banquets, after work drinks etc.
- Understand the concepts of 'saving face', loyalty, respect elders, call in/carry out favours to achieve an outcome.
- Dress well, be on time, take events seriously, and acknowledge the importance of those older/higher than you.
- Do not discuss Human Rights, Capitalism, Taiwan, Tibet etc.
- Ensure your conversations and comments do not lead to a Chinese person losing face.

Making Contacts

- Guanxi must be used when making contacts in China.
- Having a good network of connections is vital before beginning business.
- The bigger and more stable the connection base the faster business transactions will occur.
  Using a local business intermediary will help you develop local connections to those that understand the cultural complexities of multinational business.

Forms of address

- Hierarchy and the order of addressing people is very important.
- When attending a meeting ensure you line up in order or seniority so the opposite group know who to greet first.
- Make sure you also greet the group in order of seniority.
- Shake hands with anyone you are introduced to.
- A slight bow and eye contact is appreciated.
- Do not use first names. First names are reserved for members of the family, and therefore using first names will offend.

- Titles are also very important in China, therefore ensure you know your hosts official title and use it in conjunction with their surname. For example, Doctor Chen, Mrs Lee etc.
- In China, women don't change their name when they marry. They continue to use their Given or Maiden name.

Business cards

- Business cards are common within China.
- Always pass your card over with two hands, your contact details uppermost. This shows respect to those you are delivering the card too.
- Business cards should contain your contact information, and job title, but letters indicating qualifications etc can be seen as 'showy'.
- Have cards printed in English on one side and Mandarin on the other.
- Gold ink is preferred.
- Always have cards available and respect the process and information when you receive them.
- Upon receipt of a card, do not out it into a wallet or pocket, but lay it on the table during the meeting.
- At the end of the meeting treat the card with respect and store appropriately.

Body language

- Body language is subtle.
- Stillness, straight faces and limited arm movements are expected by foreigners too.
- Holding a gaze for too long is considered disrespectful, especially after among mixed sex meetings.
- Eye contact is expected upon initial greeting but not thereafter.
- Keep good posture during the duration of any meeting. Do not slouch.
- Never point with one finger.
- Physical contact is discouraged, especially amongst the older generation.
- This must be remembered in public places, but not in bus stations etc where pushing and shoving is commonplace.
- Shock, surprise and disappointment is often showed by a sharp intake of breath.

Communication styles

- Communication in China is subtle and implicit.
- Understanding the meaning behind Chinese communication is a long-term endeavour.
- The concept of 'face' or 'minx' is very important.
- 'Face' means having a high status in the eyes of their peers.
- It shows personal respect and dignity.
- 'Face' needs continuous development, to ensure that respect is gained and maintained within both business and social areas.
- 'Face' can be used like currency – given, earned, lost and removed.
- Teasing, belittling or insulting a Chinese person is always considered a very serious 'loss of face'.
- The Chinese will do almost anything to 'save face', such as avoiding commitment, not taking responsibility, withholding information and doing nothing.
- Within a conversation the Chinese will often 'skirt around an issue' if they believe that the person listening does not want to hear, or will not like the answer
- Direct questioning, frankness, negativity and abrupt responses are all seen as rude, and can result in 'loss of face'.
- Politeness is so important that you are unlikely to hear a direct 'no' response to a question. You will often hear 'I will see what I can do' which indirectly means 'no'.

- Comments and discussions are often left open indefinitely by these types of responses, so that something can be revisited later if necessary.
- Actions are often slowed down by rules, regulations and processes, so comments such as 'it is not convenient' means that the permissions etc are not currently in place and getting them will take time.
- This indirect method of communication can be very difficult to those who deal in direct communication – such as German speaking countries.
- The Chinese communication style is high context (see Low context versus high context). Relationships and behaviour are as important and the business content. Just having a great business proposal will not get you through the business process in China.
- Pay attention to the smaller elements of meetings, such as expressions (verbal and non-verbal).
- Accept the silence. Don't talk too much, and allow the Chinese and yourself, the time to think.
- Thinking is a valuable attribute in Chinese business.

Customer service and suppliers

- Guanxi ensures that relationships between suppliers and customers are continually maintained and monitored.
- There is little difference between personal and business connections, and by making the most of Guanxi will ensure that all of these relationships have a positive effect on your business dealings and will lead to further connections.
- Business connections usually evolve from other personal connections, socialising, entertaining and building trust.
- In short maintain good guanxi.

Team work

- Like many other aspects of aspects Chinese life there is a concept for work – Danwei. Each worker must participate.
- Danwei is responsible for the level of housing, health insurance, childcare, pension, employees' facilities and family provision for eating and bathing etc.
- Many workers have two or three jobs in order to maintain and suitable level of financial survival.
- Loyalty can often be found to individuals within a company rather than to the company itself – this often develops from guanxi.
- As the 'free marketplace' concept evolves within China, many employees are moving between jobs to better themselves.
- Feng Shui – the alignment and placement of items to obtain equilibrium is often followed within Chinese businesses.
- Companies use a Feng Shui professional to provide reassurance to their employees, associates and customers.
- Chinese people work well in groups, as this is the culture they have grown up in, but this does not necessarily mean they are good working together as a team.
- Individuality can be hidden by the team's requirements, meaning that foreign managers have to find innovative ways to benefit from this individuality.
- Bringing western standards and ideas rarely works, as the Chinese have grown up within a group culture, where power controls.
- To comply with western practices team managers are responsible for Best Practice, outcomes and monitoring.
- Leaders must be exceptionally strong, often along with age.
- Younger managers rarely do well, as his team will not show him the required level of respect and will not take him seriously.

Building trust

- Building trust with your work colleagues is as important as with your personal relationships.
- To do this you must visit colleagues regularly, have face to face meetings rather than virtual meeting and participate in our of work social activities.
- You must also network using the processes laid out by guanxi, the same as in developing personal connections.
- Where possible be introduced by a Chinese colleague, interpreter or intermediary.
- There is no cold calling in China.
- Remember business WILL NOT take place until a relationship has been established, regardless of who you are.

Team expectations

- Authority and order are important in China.
- Bring ambitious means to conform, use your intelligence and be energetic.
- Authoritative lines and areas of responsibility must be made and kept very clear.
- The hierarchy layout is very important to the Chinese and once given it will not be questioned.
- Bosses are expected to show their authority by making decisions for all those below him/her.
- The line of responsibility must be kept equally clear. 9
- Team members will not make decisions on their own or give their opinion as this could cause them to 'lose face'.
- The Chinese don't want to stand out from the crowd.
- Maintaining a sense of 'family' within the workplace is very important, which can in turn assist with food, childcare, health care etc.
- Think of the workplace as an extension to the family home.
- Employees expect employer involvement in their family life, as they need to feel that their manager is sensitive to their needs, be they housing, commuting, child or relationship related.

Time management

- Time is different in the Chinese workplace, as there is little short term view or urgency.
- Managers must create innovative ways to ensure that their teams hit deadlines and expectations especially within a foreign company.
- Negotiations can be difficult in terms of time. The Chinese opinion is that westerners are in a hurry. (Often true). They will slow down proceedings when it is best for them, and by bringing in a range of new connections and contacts, this slow down can be very significant, even lasting for years. However, they can also speed things up by making rapid decisions when in their best interests.

Punctuality

- Punctuality is considered a sign of respect, therefore always turn up for a meeting or event on time and dress appropriately.

Dress code

- Dress simply and conservatively.
- In larger cities and bigger businesses, shirt and tie/Dress/Trouser suits are common.

- Jackets and shirts are becoming more commonplace.
- Women should avoid shorter clothing, excessive jewellery and overwhelming perfume.
- There are no relaxed dress code days.
- Women should wear low heels, so that they are not taller than their boss.
- Wear neutral colours.
- Casually jeans are acceptable, but shorts are reserved for the gym.
- The Chinese don't like people to stand out.

Leadership styles

- Age/seniority is vital for a Chinese leader.
- Anyone young will not be taken seriously and is lower in status.
- Positions within society are generally dictated by the family you were born into and their connections.
- Things are beginning to change as people move jobs to improve their prospects and there are a small number of leaders who have worked their way into positions of power.
- Education is considered a status symbol but is dependent on the institution.
- Often, upon meeting, senior employees will give their academic credentials. An older person may give the credentials of their children, if their own studies were stopped by the cultural revolution.
- Leaders are often seen as the 'wise father', who has experience, wisdom and compassion.
- Commitment and loyalty to the company is usually nurtured by the team leader.
- Due to the huge levels of responsibility, the role of leader can be difficult to fill.
- As age is an influencing factor for a good leader, change and new technologies can be difficult to implement within Chinese business. The older generation can see the acceptable of new ideas as 'losing face'.
- Team members my make suggestions if the they believe their leader is in danger of 'losing face'.

Delegation and supervision

- Delegation can be difficult within Chinese business as the culture is based on a 'top down' system.
- Control is maintained by the top leaders.
- Delegation is only possible on a level where everyone knows exactly what is expected of them which means that delegating decisions and authority is almost impossible.
- No one is a standard team environment is able to make decisions.
- Chinese employees are taught to fit in, work within a team and not to stand out, therefore decision making or empowerment are not seen good qualities.
- In addition to 'fitting in', face also has an impact on delegation as it entails 'giving face' to another person, and putting a high level of responsibility on them, where they could 'lose face'
- Some companies have been trying to change this process but it is very slow, and difficult as it requires a deeply ingrained cultural change for the Chinese.
- Many smaller places create more flexible job descriptions to enable some responsibilities to occur throughout the team rather than on individuals.

Managing relationships

- These are extremely important in China. Business is not done unless a relationship is established.

- Face (Mianzi), Favours (Renqing) and Relationships (Guanxi) are the mainstays of social interaction.
- Guanxi has a set of rules that descend from Chinese feudal ethics (Lun) that lay out expectations of relationships between 'the noble and the humble', 'the close and the distant' and 'the individual and the group'.
- From birth the Chinese are born into a social network, then move into various others are they go through school, further education, occupation and place of residence.
- Relationships within a company requires understanding of other members of your team, the hierarchy, customers and suppliers.
- It is important to follow the rules of Guanxi and know when to call in favours. This can be a very complicated process.
- Strong leadership must be combined with diplomacy.
- Primarily respect the Chinese country and culture, your own country's laws and those of your company.
- Remember that to the Chinese the workplace is as important as their family home.

Coaching and mentoring

- There are few structured employee evaluations in china.
- Performance is based on attitude, loyalty, effort, 'Danwei' and meeting the expectations of others, rather than on measured performance.
- Giving feedback to a senior can cause them to lose face, so things that should said – aren't. This leads to frustration and lack of motivation.
- Annual appraisals often focus on elements other than the individual's objectives or achievements.
- This was of measuring performance means that coaching is new in China.
- Some foreign companies have introduced HR development and training processes into China. A few have been successful.
- Training can be found throughout many companies; however, many employees use these opportunities to go to another higher position.
- Many companies like employees who have trained elsewhere as they can reduce their own costs but offer better wages.
- Some companies require a post training commitment period to combat this behaviour.

Recruitment

- Retention is important within china. In the recent past there was a large shortfall in the amount of professional people required to work.
- Retaining good employees is a major human resources challenge facing Western employers in China.
- At one time there were about 10 openings for every one qualified employee in China - a huge shortage of professional personnel.
- The tables are now turning as millions of people are joining the professional workforce every year, and there is still a massive surplus of rural labourers.
- As the slowdown begins to hit China, unemployment may become a new issue.
- In this new employment arena, many Chinese workers are able to change jobs, and consider many other factors such as salary, employee satisfaction, work environment, etc
- Salaries are openly discussed, and most employees know the salary of their co-workers.
- Smaller companies tend to offer higher salaries to compete against the career development, prestige, and staff 'perks' offered by larger companies.
- Recruitment usually takes place via newspapers, internet, job fairs, recruitment consultants and head-hunters.

- Guanxi is also commonly used within recruitment, meaning that referrals and word of mouth are used between connections.

Motivating

- Motivation can be difficult within China, as the need for wealth and fame is not prevalent within the culture.
- Confucius taught that status, achievement and respect for others are significant signs of respect.
- Emotional displays and showing off are considered rude, so if a person is motivated by promotion and success they will often find other ways to achieve this.
- The Chinese like self-deprecation.
- The Chinese like to be part of a group and therefore the welfare of the group is of great importance but this also has to be juggled with self reward and, most importantly, saving face.
- Guanxi enables people to take advice and ask opinions of those within their connections, which may have an effect on which jobs are accepted or even applied for.
- Middle managers are the group most likely to change their job in search of self-improvement.
- The more affluent regions must concentrate on employee retention and improved talent management. Less hierarchical structures, bonuses, compensation schemes, career development are increasingly used to achieve this.
- Chinese companies also need to adjust to allow employees to reach individual achievements, rather than just for company.

Managing conflict

- Managing conflict can usually be done by following the rules of Guanxi, as Chinese workers are keen to seek advice and opinion in order to avoid trouble, or to bring harmony back to their workplace.

Interpreters

- The Chinese do not treat foreigners on equal levels, therefore a Chinese speaking colleague or interpreter is important.
- Understanding the power hierarchy and the hidden meaning within any business negotiation is key.
- Where possible use a Chinese colleague that can help you to understand the processes, meanings and expectations.
- If a Chinese colleague is not available take an interpreter.
- A good colleague or interpreter will help you read the body language.
- An interpreter or colleague should never be asked to complete negotiations or transactions alone, as the Chinese want to see the dedication, sincerity and commitment of the person/organisation they are working with.
- Using a colleague or interpreter can help Chinese negotiators to save face, and can be invaluable in conflict negotiation

Business meetings

- Meetings are held to give information, rather than place to have a discussion, brainstorm or agree on future actions.
- The leader speaks and others within the meeting listen.
- Any differences, opinions, ideas etc will have been discussed and implemented or discarded before the meetings contents were decided.
- If a meeting composes of oppositions or different team representatives, then they would expect that only one person would speak throughout the process regardless of how many attend.
- These formats are beginning to change with more involvement of multinational companies.
- If you work with the Chinese, however, make sure that you follow every process to the expected level of formality from the initial banquet to the closing of any negotiations.

Planning

- Planning meeting usually comprise of a team, of which some will have technical expertise, rather than one to one meetings.
- Ensure that the other teams know how many people from your team will be attending, so that they can bring an equivalent number, and of the same professional level.
- Before attending the meeting make sure that other participants in the meeting area ware of what you want the meeting or the process to achieve.
- Ensuring that everyone at the planning meeting is fully prepared and informed of the proceedings will lead to the meeting going well, and no one losing face.
- Be prepared for one or two meetings to be used for getting to know each other than doing business.
- If required, take an interpreter and ensure they know what your goals are for the meeting.

During

- The Chinese usually enter the meeting room in order of seniority and the most senior will speak without contradiction from other members of their team.
- The meeting will usually begin with some personal conversations, as the teams get to know each other.
- During these introductory conversations being polite is the most important aspect. You can decide whether to answer the questions or give vague responses. Do not gloat or sing your own praises. Remain humble.
- Meetings are used to describe expectations or outcomes, as the ideas, information gathering and basic process discussions will have been had prior to the meeting.
- Negative responses are rarely verbalised. Silence often means 'no', or 'there are still problems we need to consider'.
- 'Yanjiu Yanjiu', means 'we will go away, discuss and research it further and then come back to you', but implies that they are not interested in going on further with this discussion or project.
- Always ensure that any printed material can be distributed and left to everyone in the meeting, complete with translations in Chinese.

After a meeting

- Issue any additional information as requested in a timely manner.
- Review any actions required.
- If appropriate arrange for a return meeting.

Negotiating

- The Chinese follows strict protocols around negotiating as they do in all other aspects of life.
- They are extremely focused and disciplined in the way they consider new ventures and negotiate.
- They do not trust impersonal and legal processes, preferring to understand the person, the company and the expected processes before any comments or agreements can be made.
- The Chinese want to ensure that their interests and expectations are met and can be very suspicious of foreigners and their motives.
- Negotiations are always carried out by big teams and the most senior person will do the talking, as should yours.
- Chinese negotiations are based on 'soft sell, hard buy'.
- They expect large reductions, concessions and offers, so when entering into negotiations give yourself a lot of flexibility in these areas.
- Chinese negotiators often push for significant reductions by using the potential size of the market within China, but this does not always materialise.
- Once negotiations are agreed, revising is rarely possible.
- If agreements are not made the Chinese team will withdraw from discussions to reconsider and consult everyone.
- This can take a significant amount of time and can often be used as a negotiating tool. Patience is required, as Chinese negotiators are expert in 'wearing down' their counterparts.
- The Chinese team like to control the schedule and meeting locations. People who have travelled far may be reluctant to return home without a deal and can be pressured to make rash concessions.
- Attending a banquet or function the night before the negotiations can also be a tactic used.
- Showing anger is not common in China, but controlled anger can be used to make the opposing negotiators think that they are causing their Chinese counterparts to 'lose face' and lose the contract.
- Other tactics include withholding information, threatening to use rival firms, using contacts to gain further concessions, just as other negotiators.
- Guanxi and friendship is often used to benefit the Chinese side, so always make sure that the agreements are mutual and not one-sided.
- Whilst the person carrying out the negotiations may not have the final decision, they do have the power to stall and influence the process.
- Managing your own side of the negotiations is also expected.
- Ensure that you remain reserved and dignified, and the opposite would be seen as offensive and negotiations would be stopped.
- Expect the process to be slow and surrounded by red-tape and bureaucracy.
- Be prepared to give very long, detailed and knowledgeable presentations.
- Make sure you are seen making notes, so that you are perceived to be taking the process seriously.
- The Chinese note taking will be extremely accurate and if you change your message or become inconsistent, they will let you know, and the process may stall or fail.
- Make sure you do not give away sensitive information, or release concessions too quickly.
- Focus on the long-term benefits.
- Let people know why you have been chosen to do these negotiations. Do you have a specialism in working in China, or in the product etc?
- Make sure that you have an interpreter if required, and one person who knows absolutely everything about the deal.

- Be prepared to make many trips to China, or the region, keeping all travel plans flexible.
- If negotiations become difficult, be prepared to let them know that you are willing to look elsewhere.
- Competition is becoming more common amongst Chinese businesses especially producers.
- Let them know that no deal is preferable to a 'bad deal'.
- Discuss the contracts with all sides where possible to maintain consistency and ensure that everyone knows their duties and obligations.
- Make sure all wording is specific to prevent changes later after signing.
- Make sure you have enough time to study and review any deals before signing.
- Be patient and persistent. The Chinese think foreigners are often in a hurry.
- Most contracts have to be approved by political and business organisations or departments, who are not usually in communication with each other.
- Remain patient until the final approval has been received.

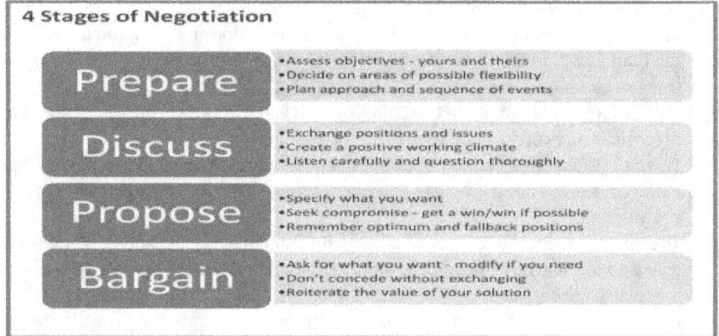

4 Stages of Negotiation

Prepare
- Assess objectives - yours and theirs
- Decide on areas of possible flexibility
- Plan approach and sequence of events

Discuss
- Exchange positions and issues
- Create a positive working climate
- Listen carefully and question thoroughly

Propose
- Specify what you want
- Seek compromise – get a win/win if possible
- Remember optimum and fallback positions

Bargain
- Ask for what you want - modify if you need
- Don't concede without exchanging
- Reiterate the value of your solution

Decision making

- The Chinese are very disciplined within their decision making processes.
- The research and discuss everything thoroughly, even by twisting and turning the conversations to find inaccuracies and inconsistencies.
- The purpose of meeting is to fact find, and the true decision maker may not ever attend.
- The lead spokesperson, however, may have great influence over the proceedings as it is usually their opinion and advice that the decision maker acts upon.
- Remain calm, patient and consistent.

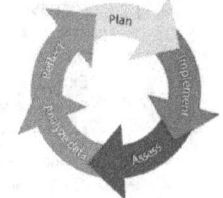

Business Presentations

Preparation

- Presentations should be factual, detailed and technically based.
- Be very knowledgeable about your product, the market, your products place in the market, your competition and your own organisation.
- Your listeners will want to know about trust and cooperation between the organisations and teams.
- Keep your presentation brief as you will be asked a lot of questions and present your information to many different groups.
- Your audience will investigate everything. You will be asked everything many times over to ensure consistency, your motives will be questioned, your product/ideas will be analysed.
- Distribute copies to everyone in the group.
- Use black and white for the hard copy and using colours can be complicated in china due to the many beliefs on colour values.
- Never exaggerate values, deadlines etc. Keep it factual.
- Within the Chinese value system, humility is a virtue.

Expectations

- Chinese people respect their elders and anyone more senior than themselves.
- Chinese people therefore do not question or challenge anyone who knows more about a subject than themselves, anyone more senior or older.
- If you require audience participation or feedback during a presentation, you must inform them of your own expectations and explain why you want it, and how it will benefit them.
- Try not to use your hands when speaking, the Chinese find it very frustrating.

Business Entertainment

- Entertaining is important in Chinese business culture as it follows the rules of, and encouraged guanxi
- It allows everyone in the process to get to know you and decide if you are worthy of doing business with.
- Remember relationships come before business so this is a step that must not be overlooked or reduced.
- Evening banquets are very common, but everything can take place at any time during the day- breakfast, lunch morning and afternoon tea etc.
- Western visits are usually treated with respect, with men and women often treated equally.
- Dinner parties are often held in restaurants or hotels.
- Make sure you are aware of the etiquette and be ready to eat some unusual dishes.
- If you do not drink, state that you don't rather than have one small drink.
- If you are a fussy eater, use a valid excuse such as allergy, medication, religion etc to ensure that your host does not lose face.
- After being invited to a dinner be ready to reciprocate as soon as possible.

Being a host

- Due to the complexity of connection building, you would be better to host according to Chinese style rather than as you would in your own country.
- The Chinese eat a vast array of food but prefer Chinese food to international food.

- If you are hosting a business dinner and Chinese food venue would be advisable.
- If you are hosting a return dinner in response to one you have already attended, ensure that yours is less imposing than theirs, or they would be in danger of losing face.
- Arrive half an hour before your guests to ensure that everything is set up and ready to receive them.
- The host takes the middle seat, facing the door.
- Everyone else should be seated in order of status with the highest person being nearest the host.
- Always follow the seating protocols.
- The host will usually order the food and drink for everyone, so everyone eats the same.
- The host will give the first toast and take the first sip of drink.
- After the toast, take some of the most expensive dish and put it on the plate of the highest status guest. This signals that eating can begin.
- Always over order, so that there will be some food left over. (saving face).
- Business will not be discussed during meals, as this is time reserved for getting to know people and establishing connections.
- Spouses or partners are not usually invited.
- Hot towels are presented after the food, signalling the end of the meal.
- Guests will leave after this, and the host must not leave until all the guests have gone.
- Tips are not given, as the host will pay for everything.
-

Being a Good Guest

- A lot of food will be served during the meal.
- A clean plate indicates that you were not fed enough.
- Not try food is considered very rude. Always try a little.
- Continually praise the food.
- Lots of toasts will be made throughout the meal, and you will be expected to make toasts in response to the hosts toast.
- "Gambei" or Kai wei" are the usual toasts at a Chinese feast.
- Raise your glass in a toast.
- Ensure you glass is full, even if only with water.
- Three glasses are usually provided, one for beer, one for soft drinks and a smaller one that is usually used for toasting. You are not expected to drink the contents of the glass during a toast. A small sip is sufficient.
- Your host is obliged to refill every empty glass, so pace yourself, or always leave some at the bottom of your glass.
- Many unusual dishes are likely to be served during a feast. If you do not wish to try delicacies such as tortoise, dog, snake skin, blood, bile, let your host know you have 'allergies'. This MUST be done before you arrive or your host will lose face.
- Being offered a chance to sign at a karaoke event means you are being accepted and given the chance to develop a better relationship.
- No matter how bad your singing, you will be rewarded with praise.

Eating out

- Chopsticks are commonly used. If you would prefer, it is OK to ask for a fork and spoon.
- Don't put your chopsticks upright in your bowl – this is a practice reserved for funerals.
- Use the rest provided to put your chopsticks down between courses.
- If you are given a communal bowl from which to take food, use the spoon provided to dish out the contents to your bowl. Never use your chopsticks. It is unhygienic.

- Don't drop or chew chopsticks.
- The Chinese are noisy eaters as this is seen as a sign of appreciation and enjoyment.
- It is OK to drink alcohol slowly, especially the more fiery drinks such as a Mao-tai.
- If you don't drink much it is OK to abstain, but just drinking one can be seen as rude.
- Tea is usually served with food.
- If you smoke, offer your cigarettes to others before lighting your own.

Invitations to a Chinese home are similar to a restaurant.

- Arrive on time, not early
- Give the hostess a gift
- Remove your shoes

Giving gifts

- Only give expensive gifts to family or very good friends as this can be seen as a bribe.
- Within business take a small gift for each member of the group.
- Leaving someone out would cause them to lose face.
- Gifts will be refused a couple of times before being accepted, and will not be opened in front of you.
- Ideal business gifts are: pens, lighters, books, painting, whisky etc.
- Ideal home visit gifts are cake or chocolate.
- Most companies have strict protocols on gift giving, so make sure you follow those as well as the expected Chinese protocols, and legal requirements in both countries.

Gift presentation is very important

- Red   Luck
- Pink/yellow   Happiness/prosperity
- White/grey/black   Reserved for funerals
- Don't give gifts in groups of four as four is associated with death.
- In mandarin the word for 'clock' is similar to the word for 'death', so avoid giving clocks as gifts.

Key Words

MANDARIN	ENGLISH
Bu dui	No
Bu xie	You're welcome
Dui	Yes
Dui bu qui	I'm sorry
Dui bu qui (pronounce Doi bu chi)	Excuse me
Duo shao qian?	How much?
Gan Bei	Cheers ('Bottoms up, empty your glass')
Guanxi	Connections, relationships
Hao	Fine (good)
Hua Qiao	Overseas Chinese
Jia Ting	Extended family, very close friends
Jingli	Manager
Naixin	Patience
Ni hao	Hello
Ni hao ma/ Ni chifan le ma	How are you? ('have you eaten yet?')
Qing	Please
Wang shang hao	Good evening
Wei	Hello (on phone)
Wo bu dong	I don't understand
Wo jiao...	My name is...
Wu an	Good afternoon
Xie-xie (pronounce sh ee eh -sh ee eh)	Thank you
Zai jian	Goodbye
Zao an	Good morning
Zhong Guo	China/Chinese
Zhuren	Director
Zhuxi	Chairman
Zongjingli	General manager

CULTURAL DIMENSIONS

Cultural profile

The cultural profile graph gives a visual indication of potential differences between cultures. By including another culture to the graph, you would be able to identify and be aware of major differences and also similarities. Understanding the differences means that you can change your communication style to avoid conflict.

This graph shows the typical profile of a Chinese national, and although everyone is uniquely different, comparing typical profiles gives you an awareness of the differences you could encounter, and enables you to be better prepared.

For example, a British national moving to China will have to change from thinking about their own place in a team, to thinking about how the team works, improves and delivers. Relationships are far more important the individual tasks.

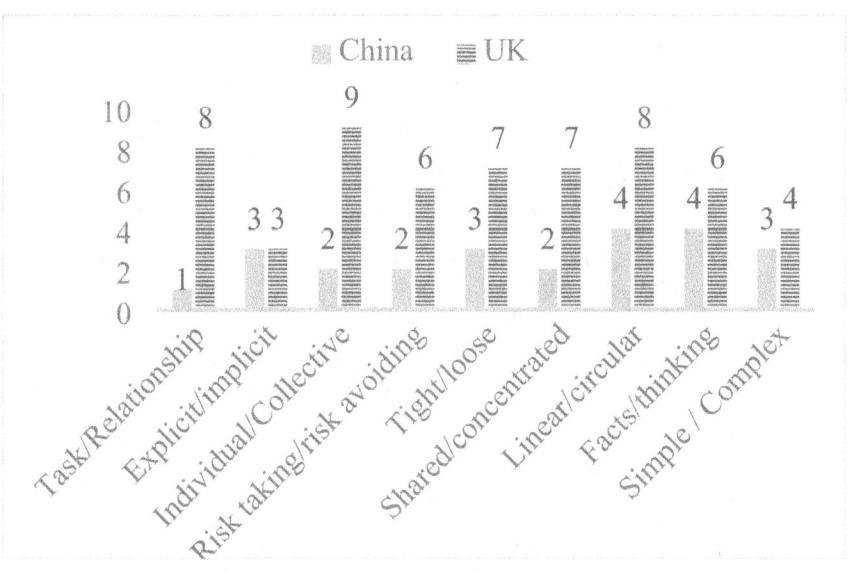

Task versus relationship

TASK

Impersonal. Let's get down to business.

Rules before relationship.

Things get done when the right plans and processes are in place.

"I have an appointment to visit the museum with Fred. I must be there by 2pm.

Accomplishments, and responsibility leads to success.

Decisions made by individuals. Often a quick process

RELATIONSHIP

Can I trust you? Are you loyal? Things get done when the right relationships are in place

"I am spending time with Fred today. Maybe go to the museum"

Maintaining relationships, good judgement, social skills and loyalty leads to success.

Decisions made by the group – can be wide ranging

- Relationships are key within China.
- Who you know and the relationship you have with them is very important.
- Understanding of "Guanxi" is important. It is the relationship network.
- Networks tend to be very complex and intricate.
- Go-betweens are often used to help the development of these relationships, especially if the two parties are unknown to each other.
- Negotiations and favours are always reciprocal. They can transcend people and generations.
- Family is the key framework behind "Guanxi" and usually incorporates extended relationships, including business and social contacts.
- Relationship structures are arranged according to Confucius going from young up to old.
- Younger members of community are expected to care for the older members.
- Trust and reliability must be developed and proved before business communications begin.
- The first meeting will rarely discuss business matters.
- Understanding the person, you wish to work with is vital.
- Morals and ethics take priority over anything legal.
- The impact on wider levels, such as the community, the future, other relationships, duties and expectations will be considered along with the original proposal.
- Government bodies and officials are often consulted.
- Business, money and success are great motivators in china, and are taken seriously, despite relationship expectations.

This can affect
- Sales and marketing
- Recruitment
- Contracts
- Building trust

Direct versus Indirect

Say what you mean. Mean what you say

Literal truthfulness is valued within a business environment.

Often linked to task-based cultures.

Saying 'no' or 'I don't know' is viewed as honest.

Business conversations rarely taken personally.

Meaning often has to be taken from body language and inference, as well as words.

Direct communication is seen as impolite or rude.

Often linked to relationship-based cultures.

Yes, is often used to show willingness or politeness, even if it cannot be achieved.

Any conversation can lead to embarrassment.

- Confucian values are still very important within China.
- Modesty, humility, harmony and respect for others are key Confucian values.
- These values are reflected heavily within the Chinese language.
- Traditional Chinese is very formal and implicit, but this is changing in some of the more modern cities.
- 'Face' is still very important in China. This is the level of respect and reverence held by others about you.
- Bad 'face' comes about from being over-opinionated, being critical in public, shamed, or disrespectful.
- Good 'face' will result in praise, recognition, admiration and deference.
- Chinese feelings are kept subdued with them rarely being shown ion the surface.
- Public displays of emotion are not shown in public, and are viewed as immature.
- There is usually a marked difference between private at home thoughts and comments, and public comments.
- The Chinese language depends on the tone of voice for understanding and this can made them appear abrupt and even rude. This is not their intention.
- The huge range of vocabulary choice in Chinese can also make them appear vague, as they to search for the correct word, and not cause any offense.
- Negative responses, phrase or comments are discouraged, instead silence will save 'face' and prevent any value confusion.
- Pauses and silences in the language can also cause confusion.
- The length of pauses and silences is very long, and many westerners can find themselves feeling very uncomfortable

This can affect
- Negotiating
- Coaching and supporting
- Conflict management
- Information sharing

The Individual versus the collective

INDIVIDUAL

Me before we.

Less consideration of the past and the present. The future is important.

Competition

Individual achievement is important.

Study and hard work are rewarded.

Spending on assets is encouraged to show success.

COLLECTIVE

We before me.

Tradition and customs are very important.

Collaboration.

The success of the group is very important.

Position is given.

Spending in the form of gifts and celebrations is important.

- A society that works best for the group.
- Conscious says that each person has a key place in society.
- Respect is given the all elders.
- Everyone belongs to china.
- China is the oldest civilisation in the world, and its inhabitants are very proud of this.
- Traditional labour was agricultural within closely knit communities.
- Communism promoted and encouraged this.
- During the cultural revolution individuality and self-expression were subdued and discouraged.
- For a long time, families were only allowed to have one child.
- Sharing and equality is still very important in Chinese life.
- In negotiations the stronger side is expected to support the weaker side.
- In monetary terms the poorer side should expect support from the richer side.
- In international negotiations the Chinese often see themselves as poorer.
- This can have serious consequences for organisations and individuals entering into business negotiations with Chinese nationals and organisations.

This can affect
- Teamwork
- Motivation
- Feedback
- Decision making

Risk taking versus risk avoiding

RISK TAKING

Make change happen; act decisively. New is good.

High tolerance for uncertainty.

Higher levels of innovation and change.

Flexible attitude to deadlines (usually shorter).

More informal or spontaneous activities and projects.

May be many different elements to a project at one time.

RISK AVOIDING

Avoid change. Steady, but sure. Stress continuity.

Low tolerance to uncertainty.

Loyalty is encouraged.

Traditional gender roles

Projects, processes etc. are well planned.

Rules, regulation and legislation

- The Chinese are very risk averse.
- They distrust anyone they don't know regardless of nationality.
- Chinses history has made them very wary of foreigners as they have spent many years under foreign rule and separated from the rest of the world.
- Foreigner in Mandarin is 'yang guizi' (foreign devil).
- Chairman Mao's government imprisoned those with foreign connections and objected to free speech.
- These two elements combined have led to the Chinese being suspicious and fearful of anyone they don't know.
- Chinese protocol dictates that there are correct behaviours for social and business environments.
- These protocols are taught very early in school and continue through to adult life.
- The Chinese are taught not to question authority.
- They believe that the authorities know best and will do what is right.
- Spontaneity and independence are discouraged. This includes brainstorming, collective thought and creative thinking.
- Standing out from the crowd is seen as a risk, and most likely to lead to loss of face.
- A Chinese proverb says – "the careful ones don't make mistakes".
- Due to international business requirements, those that live in eastern cities are most likely to be entrepreneurial and risk takers.

This can affect
- Controlling
- Investing
- Managing change
- Planning

Urgent versus relaxed

URGENT

Be Punctual, control time. Time is money.

Complete one section before moving on to the next.

Rapport/relationship building is not important, unless it can be done quickly.

Tight timescales and deadlines are key to good business

RELAXED

Be Flexible, go with the flow. Things will happen in their own time.

Information, sections and decisions can be revisited and repeated many times.

Time should be taken to build a good rapport, to allow a relationship to develop.

Timescales are rarely issued and more rarely achieved.

- Time and punctuality are often dependant on the level of the relationship.
- Long standing relationship are more valued than shorter ones, so an engagement with one them will take priority over anything else, regardless of time planned.
- Accessing people through networks and connections is vital if business is to be successful.
- Developing business relationships are very time consuming and complex.
- Decisions are long winded, and many people will need consulting, including government organisations, family members and a variety of other organisations.
- Business decisions often involve levels that would not normally speak to each other, so intermediaries and communicators are involved.
- Patience and persistence is needed.
- Planning is not common in china, with things often being limited to two weeks in advance.
- This is due to the complexity in getting things arranged only to have them cancelled.
- Negotiators often manipulate the situation between different parties depending on the requirements involved. They can test patience and character by taking their time but can also test commitments by speeding things up.

Areas of impact
- Scheduling
- Meeting deadlines
- Project management
- appointments

Power equality versus power distance

POWER EQUALITY

Distribute power and authority within the group – collective.

A belief that everyone should have the same opportunity to succeed.

You often know the person who makes decisions.

Subordinates and decision makers are interdependent.

People are ready and expected to approach and/or contradict their superiors.

Everyone has privileges

POWER DISTANCE

Focus power and authority on specific people in the group – centralised.

A belief that your personal distance from power is a fact of life that rarely changes

Subordinates are dependent on decision makers.

People are not equal and everyone has their place.

The powerful have privileges.

- Control and power comes from the top.
- This strict order goes back to Confucius' time.
- Emperors and dictators have ruled China for most of its existence before the communist party took control.
- Power is pyramidal, with the main power being at the top and then filtered down through a strict structure.
- "guanxi" is used to gain access to those at the top through networking and generating connections that will eventually to those in power.
- However, the Chinese distrust of anyone they do not know also extends to this powerful hierarchy.
- The rules and regulations generated by this powerful elite, are often broken or ignored.
- The power held by the few is almost impossible to enforce amongst the masses.
- Corruption is common, and illegal businesses are thriving.
- International and global business need to get government approval before proceeding, but they also need to get the local government and officials onside too.
- Management and leadership is given from the top down.
- Leaders to be respected and not questioned.
- 'Face' must be maintained at all costs.
- Commitment, loyalty and age are to be rewarded.
- Connections and networks are more important than titles and job descriptions.

This can affect
- Organising
- Leading
- Delegating
- Decision making

Linear versus circular

<u>LINEAR</u>

Analytical step by step process toward solution.

Western culture.

Lines divide – man/nature, subject/object, mind/matter

Individuality – goals, perspectives, interest, achievements.

Future – the past has happened and the present is uncontrollable.

<u>CIRCULAR</u>

Focus on exploring and integrating perspectives in a relatively unstructured way.

Eastern/Chinese culture.

Circles enclose –interdependence, relativity and integration.

Integrity – community, harmony, group objectives, safeguarding.

Tradition – the past loops and repeats, therefore it should be respected and learnt from.

- Thoroughness is very important to the Chinese.
- Making sure that anyone or anything that is likely to be affected by any deal or business venture is consulted and/or considered.
- Where at all possible they want a consensus/agreement from anyone involved within the negotiations.
- This means that negotiations, can be halted for these other areas to be consulted and considered, and then there will inevitably be spurs off these side negotiations to consult more of the potentially affected.
- In addition to this rigorous consultation period, bureaucracy can be complicated, extensive and time consuming.
- As high context communicators, some information may seem trivial to those outside the culture, but it is vital that anyone wishing to do business in China accepts, and, if possible, embraces the process.
- Every meeting and piece of communication will be documented to be kept as evidence, therefore consistency is important. Many find it help to keep their own detailed records.
- Records will be referred to and re-referred to, even if some area of the negotiations have been previously discarded or previously agreed.
- Contracts never last their agreed time, as any changes in circumstances, environment etc, will require a new contract.
- Renewing a contract requires the same patience as negotiating a new contract. Previous agreement or work relations doesn't mean preferential treatment.
- Due to the length of time involved, there are often multiple negotiations happening at any one time. This may include many companies looking for the same or similar outcomes.
- Pitching one company against another is common in China.

This can affect
- Standardisation
- Problem solving
- Implementation
- Meetings
- management

Concrete versus abstract

CONCRETE
Emphasis on data and concrete experiences.

Does not often reflect or consider areas outside of process or procedure.

Projects are carried out one at a time.

Change is not expected after the process has begun.

Fact

ABSTRACT
Emphasis on reasoning, concepts and logic.

Reflect on events, attributes, relationships and potential outcomes.

Uses different scenarios to create different environments.

Planning and running multiple projects is usual.

Outcome can be different to the plan. Change is expected.

Thought.

- Consistency is important in China, so repeated questioning is common.
- Weak links are not welcome within negotiations, therefore the Chinese will repeatedly question motives and methods etc, to find them.
- Keep your own ideas and notes consistent and achievable.
- The importance of everything is in the detail. Therefore, all methods, viewpoints and possible outcomes will be considered.
- Moral and ethical considerations may appear more important that legal issues, but this can be dependent on the organisation, and location.
- Chinese companies may be very interested in the people working within the business, including issues like their own morals and ethical views, as well as their roles, and experience.
- Anyone giving a presentation or leading negotiations is expected to be very knowledgeable about the project or proposition.
- Chinese culture is led from the top down, and therefore anyone representing the company in China, must have the answers.
-

This can affect
- Data gathering
- Evaluation
- Problem analysis
- persuading

Low context versus high context

LOW
Reduce to basics. Focus on essentials with
little context.

Societal connections are shorter and there
are many.

Expected behaviours do have to be
explained.

Wider networks with defined roles and tasks.

Cultural knowledge is spoken of.

simple

HIGH

Focus on developing a detailed, contextual
understanding.

Societal connections have been developed
over very many years.

Explicit cultural behaviour is not needed, as
everyone knows.

Complicated, multi-topic networks based on
relationships.

Cultural Knowledge is known.

complex

- The Chinese culture has been carefully developed over many centuries, meaning that the way they live their life has been evolved and honed to their needs.
- The Chinese believe their culture is logical and beneficial.
- Confucius and Tao have had a huge influence over Chinese culture, and these factors make the Chinese culture a complex one.
- You are expected to know the intricacies of the culture, and few people will explain elements to you, as they are so ingrained within the society that behaviour is automatic.
- Most major economies have simple cultural structures, so the Chinese culture can be quite a challenge.
- This complexity can be seen within their decision-making as they will often provide a variety of options rather than focusing on one.
- Many Chinese are being educated to a very high level and are learning a range of languages that will be well suited to international business.
- The younger Chinese also enjoy debates and discussions, especially over politics and business.
- Business negotiations will not take a linear route, with issues being rejected and then revisited, and vice versa.
- The Chinese love China, and will always prefer to negotiate, and entertain in China.

This can affect
- Knowledge transfer
- Report and memo writing
- Presentations
- Making proposals

CHINESE DYNASTIES

2205BC – 1766 BC	Xia (Hsia)
1766BC – 1122BC	Shang
1020 BC-771 BC	Western Zhou - Spring and Autumn Period
770 BC-404 BC	Eastern Zhou
403 BC-222 BC	Warring States
221 BC-206 BC	Qin (Ch'in) - China Unified under centralized bureaucracy
206 BC-23 AD	Western Han
25-220	Eastern Han
220-280	Three Kingdoms
265-316	Western Jin (Chin)
317-420	Eastern Jin
420-581	Southern and Northern Dynasties
581-618	Sui
618-907	Tang
907-960	Five Dynasties and Ten Kingdoms
960-1127	Northern Song (Sung)
1127-1279	Southern Song
1279-1368	Yuan (Mongol)
1368-1644	Ming
1644-1912	Qing (Manchu)

MODERN HISTORY

Twentieth Century Events

1912	Qing Dynasty overthrown by Guomindang and Sun Yat-sen
1921	Chinese communist party vs Chiang Kaishek
1934-35	The Long March, led by Mao Zedong
1937	Full scale Japanese invasion
1949	Chinese communists seize power as Nationalists flee to Taiwan
1949	Stock Market closed.
1958	The Great Leap Forward: millions moved on collectivist farms, 25-30 million die in famine
1966-1976	Cultural Revolution: Red guards purge 60% of party officials (Mao suppressed elites)
1976-1998	Deng Xaioping's relatively liberal rule and economic reforms
1980-81	China admitted to the IMF and World Bank
1980-82	Deng Xiaoping supports capitalist techniques for building Chinese socialism
1989	Student demonstrations, Tiananmen Square riots, troops killing several hundred protesters
1990 – December	Shanghai Stock Market reopens
1997	Hong Kong handed back to China
2001 - November	China enters the WTO (World Trade Organisation)
2003	SARS outbreak damages tourism industry. Jintao Hu becomes President
2004 - November	China signs a landmark trade agreement with 10 south-east Asian countries.
2007 -April	During a landmark visit, Wen Jiabao becomes the first Chinese prime minister to address Japan's parliament. Both sides agree to try to iron out differences over their shared history.
2008 – May	A massive earthquake hits Sichuan province, killing tens of thousands.
2008 - November	The government announces a $586 billion stimulus package to avoid the economy slowing.
2009 - February	Russia and China sign $25bn deal to supply China with oil for next 20 years in exchange for loans. Hillary Clinton calls for deeper US-China partnership on first overseas tour as secretary of state.
2009 – July	Scores of people are killed and hundreds injured in the worst ethnic violence in decades as a protest in the restive Xinjiang region turns violent. First sign of relaxation of strictly enforced one-child policy, as officials in Shanghai urge parents to have a second child in effort to counter effects of ageing population. Leaders of China and Taiwan exchange direct messages for the first time in more than 60 years.
2009 – October	China stages mass celebrations to mark 60 years since the Communist Party came to power. Six men are sentenced to death for involvement in ethnic violence in Xinjiang.
2009 – December	China executes Briton Akmal Shaikh for drug dealing, despite pleas for clemency from the British government.
2010 – January	China posts a 17.7% rise in exports in December, suggesting it has overtaken Germany as the world's biggest exporter. The US calls on Beijing to investigate the cyber-attacks, saying China has tightened censorship. China condemns US criticism of its internet controls.
2010 – March	The web giant Google ends its compliance with Chinese internet censorship and starts re-directing web searches to a Hong Kong, in response to cyber-attacks on e-mail accounts of human rights activists.

2010 – September	Diplomatic row erupts over Japan's arrest of Chinese trawler crew in disputed waters in East China Sea. Japan later frees the crew but rejects Chinese demands for an apology.
2010 - October	Jailed Chinese dissident Liu Xiaobo is awarded Nobel Peace Prize, prompting official protests from Beijing. Vice-President Xi Jinping named vice chairman of powerful Central Military Commission, in a move widely seen as a step towards succeeding President Hu Jintao.
2011 - February	China formally overtakes Japan to become the world's second-largest economy after Tokyo published figures showing a Japanese GDP rise of only four per cent in 2010.
2011 - April	Arrest of Chinese artist and activist Ai Weiwei for "economic crimes" sparks international campaign for his release. He is freed after more than two months' detention.
2011 July-August	Police kill seven Uighurs suspected of being behind separate attacks in the towns of Horan and Kashgar blamed on separatists.
2011 - November	Authorities present outspoken artist Ai Weiwei with $2.3m tax demand, which is paid by donations from his supporters.
2011 - December	Southern fishing village of Wukan comes to international attention after violent protests by locals against land seizures by officials. Authorities respond by sacking two local officials and agreeing to villagers' key demands. China issues new rules requiring users of microblogs to register personal details.
2012 - January	Official figures suggest city dwellers outnumber China's rural population for the first time. Both imports and exports dip, raising concern that the global economic slowdown could be acting as a drag on growth.
2012 - March	Chongqing Communist Party chief Bo Xilai is dismissed on the eve of the Party's ten yearly leadership change, in the country's biggest political scandal for years. His wife is placed under investigations over the death of British businessman Neil Heywood in the city in November
2012 - April	China ups the limit within which the yuan currency can fluctuate to 1% in trading against the US dollar, from 0.5%. The US welcomes the move, as it has been pressing China to let the yuan appreciate.
2012 - August	Gu Kailai, the wife of disgraced politician Bo Xilai, is given a suspended death sentence after admitting to murdering British businessman Neil Heywood. State media for the first time link Bo himself to the scandal.
2012 - September	Disgraced politician Bo Xilai is expelled from the Communist Party over accusations of abuse of power and corruption, in a move seen as burying his political career. A month later, he is expelled from parliament and prosecutors open a criminal investigation against him. 2012 November Communist Party holds congress expected to start a once-in-a-decade transfer of power to a new generation of leaders. Vice President and heir-apparent Xi Jinping takes over as party chief and assumes the presidency in March 2013. 2013 January A Tibetan monk receives a suspended death sentence and his nephew 10 years in jail for inciting eight people to burn themselves to death. Tibetan activists say they were forced to confess. Nearly 100 Tibetans have set themselves on fire since 2009, many fatally, in apparent protest at Chinese rule. 2013 February Japan's Prime Minister Shinzo Abe calls the decision by a Chinese frigate to put a radar lock on a Japanese navy ship a "dangerous act" that could lead to an unpredictable situation". China says Japan should stop "illegal" activities near a group of Japanese controlled islands over which both countries, plus Taiwan, claim sovereignty. 2013 March Vice-President and Communist Party chief Xi Jinping takes over as resident, completing the once-in-a-decade transfer of

	power to a new generation of leaders. He launches an efficiency and anti-corruption drive, exemplified by the dissolution of the powerful railways ministry. New Premier Li Keqiang says sustainable economic growth will remain top priority.
2013 - August	Two ethnic Uighur men are sentenced to death over clashes in Xinjiang in April that left 21 people dead, according to Beijing. There was more violence in Xinjiang in June, which China attributed to Islamists.
2013 - Sept	Former senior leader Bo Xilai is sentenced to life in prison for bribery, embezzlement and abuse of power in the most politically charged trial in China in decades.
2013 - October	A car drives into a crowd and catches fire in Tiananmen Square in Beijing, killing five. Authorities suspect it was an attack by Uighur separatists.
2013 - November	Communist Party leadership announces plans to relax one-child policy, in force since 1979. Other reforms include the abolition of "re-education through labour" camps. China says it has established a new Air Defence Identification Zone (ADIZ) over an area of the East China Sea, covering disputed islands controlled by Japan and a disputed South Korean-controlled rock. Japan and South Korea both protest against the move, and the US voices concern.
2013 - December	China successfully lands the Yutu ("Jade Rabbit") robotic rover on the surface of the moon, the first soft landing there for 37 years.
2014 - January - May	Attacks in Xinjiang Region and elsewhere in China, focused on markets and railway stations and attributed to Uighur separatists, leave tens of people dead and more injured.
2014 - January	China allows foreign companies majority ownership of some telecom and internet services in the Shanghai free trade zone.
2014 - February	China's trade surplus jumps to $31.9bn (£19.4bn) - up 14 per cent from a year earlier-easing concerns the world's second largest economy may be stuck in a slowdown. 2014 March Chinese e-commerce giant Alibaba and China's largest Twitter-like service Weibo unveils plans to sell shares on the US stock market.
2014 - May	The US charges five Chinese army officers with industrial cyber-espionage, in the first case of its kind. China signs a 30-year deal worth an estimated $400bn for gas supplies from Russia's Gazprom
2014 - December	Senior economy ex-official Liu Tienan jailed for life in multi-million-dollar bribery scandal, as part of official anti-corruption campaign. Was deputy head of National Development and Reform Commission until dismissal in August 2013.
2015 – June	The Chinese stock market bubble burst, losing over one third of its value by February 2016. The worst day of trading was 27th July
2015 – September	China history day parade was held in Tiananmen Square, to celebrate 70th anniversary of victory over Japan during WWII
2016 – September	Tiangong 2, a Chinese space laboratory, was launched.
2016 – September	The G20 summit was held in Hangzhou. The first summit held in china.

FURTHER INFORMATION

This guide was produced by ChatterBox. ChatterBox are specialists in Business English and Relocation.

Our advisers are specialists within the Business English field and also include an MBA Consultant. The focus on adapting to culture and communication emerged when many of our English learners encountered difficulty in adapting to new cultures despite speaking the local language.

By understanding the key values of the country you are living and working in, you are able to understand and adapt to some of the differences that you will experience. This will make you a much better communicator and feel that you are able to integrate with your new environment, rather than live on the edge or leave the country completely.

If you would like more materials please visit:

www.chatterboxenglish.com

Or contact us on:

Hello@chatterboxenglish.com

Better Integration

In order to integrate as quickly and painlessly as possible, it is best to compare your own personal culture with your chosen country.

If you would like to get an extra country profile, please email hello@chatterboxenglish.com .

www.ingramcontent.com/pod-product-compliance
Lightning Source LLC
Chambersburg PA
CBHW071151220526
45468CB00003B/1017